THE BOWHUNTER'S TIP BOOK

by Bob Marchand

Canadian Cataloguing in Publication Data

Marchand, Bob 1949
The Bowhunter's Tip Book

Includes index.
ISBN 0-9680571-2-8

1. Bowhunting. 1 Title
SK36.M37 1997   799.2'028'5   C96-910814-1

ISBN 0-9680571-2-8 (Soft cover)

Published by: B.S. Publications

                       P.O. Box 2953
                       Kelowna, British Columbia
                       V1X4K5

Printed in Canada

THE BOWHUNTER'S TIP BOOK

This book was written after many requests from bowhunters who read *The Hunters Tip Book.*

You will find that this book is filled with tips that will enhance the abilities of anyone interested in the sport of bowhunting. It offers a better understanding of the methods and equipment available to the bowhunter.

Twenty years of bowhunting knowledge and experience has been compiled in this book to make your hunting experience more fulfilling and enjoyable.

Photographs are included of animals harvested by the members of the Marchand family with their archery equipment. The photos are of the author, his son Chad and the authors brother Rick.

Acknowledgements

This book would not have been possible without the help of the bowhunting friends that I have come to know and hunt with during my many years of bowhunting across North America.

I would especially like to thank my family who stuck by me when times got hard. They put up with a lot and they deserve much recognition and more.

Special thanks to Vee Toffolo who did an excellent job on the art work in this book. Thank you, Vee

The cover of this book was made possible by the fine people at Skyline Camo. It goes to show you that they know what they are doing when it comes to camouflage.

This book is designed to help the novice and experienced bowhunter by teaching them "just the tips". In this way a lot more of their time can be spent bowhunting instead of learning from their own mistakes.

It is my hope that you enjoy this book and take it into the context that it was intended.

Bob Marchand

This book is dedicated to my lovely wife Sally -

My inspiration and partner

About The Author

Bob Marchand has spent most of his life in the Northern Woods of Ontario in the small town of Kapuskasing.   His family was raised on the benefits of wild game and moose meat.

Most of his time was spent exploring and learning the secrets that the woods had to offer.

When Bob was 23 years old he joined the City of Timmins Police Force. During this time he started a small bowhunting based business and as well became involved in outfitting.

He obtained his pilots license and logged many hours of float time on the northern lakes.

Bob was retired from the police force on a disability pension after a shooting incident and continued his love for the outdoors.

In 1985 he was named one of Ontario's top three moose bowhunters by *Ontario Out of Doors (magazine)*.

In 1993 he moved to British Columbia where he now resides.

Active in all outdoor interests, he was involved in many various organizations. He was a member of the Northern Ontario Tourist Outfitters Assoc, North Eastern Director for the Federation of Ontario Bowhunters, President and founder of the Timmins Bowhunters Inc. and the Kapuskasing Bowhunters. He was the

owner/operator of Tri - ouR - Outfitters and is a regular member of the Professional Bowhunters Society. He is also a qualified International Bowhunter Education Instructor. Now in British Columbia, Bob is the President of the Traditional Bowhunters of British Columbia.

Bob has written many articles for various outdoor publications and goes by the pen name "The Jungle Cat"

TABLE OF CONTENTS

Bowhunting Tips

Tree Stand Tips

TABLE OF CONTENTS

Bowhunting Answers

Clothes For The Bowhunter

Gifts For The Bowhunter

CHAPTER ONE
Bowhunting Tips

BOWHUNTING TIPS

☐ Have you ever been in a situation where you felt that you could rattle a whitetail buck in from its feeding or bedding area but you do not have any rattling horns with you?
Why not try using the arrows in your bow quiver?
Take an arrow and strike it on the remaining arrows in your quiver. Do so in a manner that imitates the sound of horns clashing. Pounding your feet on the ground while you are doing this will also help by sounding like the stomping of the bucks hoofs while they are fighting.

☐ Most bowhunters will practice all summer with their archery equipment and when the fall comes they are very accurate indeed. As summer ends and the fall hunting season comes, the practice stops and the hunting starts. The trouble is this. The shooting stops because they are spending too much time hunting. This often results in a less than perfect shot and can increase your workload in tracking a wounded animal down. Try to bring a practice arrow in your quiver with your regular hunting arrows. As you walk along during your hunt you can take that practice shot going into or out of your hunting location. The shot can also be taken before leaving your tree stand. If you place a metal blunt on the end of your hunting arrow you can also use it for hunting small game.

☐ Ever go out hunting early in the morning and missed that first shot? Why not try this?

Every morning as soon as you get dressed and before you go to work, school or wherever, go into your back yard and fire one single arrow with your bow at a practice butt changing the target distance daily. Put your bow down and leave the arrow there and go to work. When you come back, retrieve the arrow and then practice if you so desire. By taking this first shot every morning you are actually training yourself to place that first arrow in the morning in the perfect spot. Try this. It works.

PRACTICE, EVALUATE YOUR SKILLS AND SHOOT ACCORDINGLY

☐ Here's a word of warning from something that I have had happen to one of my friends and it could easily happen to you.

On very cold wet days after hunting and you are driving home with your bow strung in the front of your vehicle. Be aware that turning on the vehicle heater full on the floor to keep warm is not the brightest thing to do. The heat from the vehicle's heater if hot enough can and will affect the glue which holds the limb separations together. If your bow is strung and the limbs are in the path of the heat it can separate the glue in the limbs causing the bow to come apart, distorted and useless.

☐ If you want to go hunting for turkey, geese or ducks with your bow it is best to use small game stoppers behind the broadhead. This will give your arrow the power to harvest the birds by using both penetration and impact. The purpose of this is to keep the arrow in the bird so that it will obstruct its movements allowing you a better chance to retrieve it. If you do not want to pay the price for these turkey stoppers why not try to make some home made ones? Find an old thick rubber tube from a large truck or Skidder tire. Something that is fairly thick yet flexible. Take a six or seven inch section of 1/2 inch copper pipe and sharpen the edges. Use it as a punch to poke out half inch sections of the tube. Punch out as many as you want. Now poke the tube rounds out of the copper piping and then take an empty 38 Cal. casing or 9 mm. and use them to punch the center out of these small 1/2 inch pieces of tubing. The result makes the rubber shape look like a miniature donut. Remove the broadhead and slide the rubber stopper over the end of the arrow and then reinstall the broadhead. If you are hunting thin skinned animals such as squirrels, rabbits or grouse etc, you can use a metal blunt and slide the rubber stopper behind it.

OBEY GAME LAWS

☐ Why spend extra hard earned hunting cash on metal blunts to hunt small game with. Simply slide an empty pistol casing over the business end of your arrow. They are just as effective as metal blunts and offer the same results when it impacts small game.

You will find that the best compatible shell casings are 357, 38 cal, and 9 mm.

Chad Marchand with his limit of bow harvested partridge

☐ For those of you who use bow sights while hunting why not consider this? Your pins are usually set at 10, 20, 30 and 40 yards. These sight pins have probably been measured out under ideal situations on a measured range. What happens when you are in the field and you bump your sights knocking them out of whack? With no tape measure you will not be really assured of the distance to resight your pins.

Why don't you pace off the distances and set your pins according to your pace. In this way you can resight your pins in the field and continue hunting.

Further to this, to help you estimate your yardage. Why not take a walk anywhere, anytime and estimate what you take to be the distances of 10, 20, 30, and 40 yards and pace them off. See how close you are. Then continue to do this at the different distances as you walk along. You will be surprised at how fast you can accurately estimate the distance which in turn will help you pick the right sight pin when that animal comes into range.

..

RAZOR SHARP BROADHEADS + HEAVY ARROWS = BETTER PENETRATION

☐ Many bow hunters have difficulty picking a spot on the animal when it comes down to the shot.

Here is a way to train yourself to pick a spot.

Every animal that you look at, be it your dog, cat, horse

or whatever, concentrate on a spot in the lung area. Do this enough times and you will soon find out that this spot will come to you instantly every time you look at an animal. When the moment of truth comes you will automatically pick that spot and you will be able to put a well placed arrow in its boiler room.

☐ If you are concerned about scent on your trail when you are hunting, remember that animals cannot smell rubber. Keep this in mind while hunting with your bow near game trails, scrapes etc. Try not to wear your leather boots. Everything that you touch while in the bush such as trees, grass and shrubs will have the scent of your clothes and body odor pushed into the foliage and make them a source of human smell for the animals to detect.

TAKE YOUR KIDS BOWHUNTING AND YOU WON'T BE HUNTING FOR YOUR KIDS

☐ If you ever wondered where a good spot would be to set up an ambush for whitetails. Check in locations where there are deer trails that go up hill. Follow it to a bench like area and where the trail starts to go horizontal to the mountain. This trail will most likely lead to a thicket. You can usually be assured that the location is probably a bedding area. It would be a good idea to set up a stand just outside of it to ambush a whitetail buck as he leaves his bedding area.   ..14..

☐ If you ever hit an animal and want to know how soon you should go after it, here is a guideline for you to follow which may help you out:

A lung, or heart shot hit, wait at least fifteen minutes.

A gut shot, wait at least six hours. The animal will lay down and stiffen up allowing you to track and harvest the animal. Gut shot or liver hit deer will often run with their back hunched up.

A hit in the ham or leg means that the animal should be pushed as soon as possible to allow it to bleed out faster.

☐ If tracking an animal at night you will find that using a gas lantern is best. The shiny blood will be reflected by the light.

KEEP YOUR BROADHEADS RAZOR SHARP

☐ If you wish to determine the location of the hit of your animal, here are several suggestions.

Frothy blood which has bubbles in it usually indicates a lung shot.

Thick blood with bubbles in it may indicate a hit in the windpipe.

A gut shot usually has food materials and blood combined and your arrows would be strong smelling.

Dark, red blood on your arrow or on the ground is a good indication of a hit in the liver.

If, when following a blood trail you notice that there is blood on both sides of the trail this indicates to you that the arrow was a pass through and means that there is an entrance and exit hole.

A check for hair at the scene can also indicate the location of the hit. For example; if you find white hair on the ground or on your arrow you can picture where the shot hit was, such as the white portion of a deer's neck or belly.

☐ Very often fatally hit animals will head towards water or thick cover. If you lose your blood trail, try checking out nearby rivers or ponds. Many times bears will crawl under thick branches of trees to expire and they are difficult to spot. Mark the last area that you lost the trail with a piece of toilet paper. Then work a grid pattern from that point in an effort to pick up the trail or locate the animal. Toilet paper is easy to spot and is biodegradable.

☐ Have you ever had to walk into your tree stand area at night and had to carry your flashlight with you, lighting up the whole area? This is very reasonable and smart. However, many conservation officers frown on this. They can, and sometimes will, charge you with hunting at night or pit lamping.

In order to rectify this, it would be advisable to use a

small pen light flashlight such as the mini-mag. These small units are extremely powerful and a conservation officer would look pretty silly in court in front of a judge showing him a six inch flashlight and accusing you of pit lamping.

☐ If you have found a game trail and have ever wondered what direction the animals are heading in. Why not keep a spool of thread in your pocket and tie it across the game trail? The animal will unknowingly walk through it breaking the thread and the thread will always point in the direction that the animal was travelling.

☐ Ever stumble around in the dark trying to find your way to or from your tree stand? Flagging tape can be hard to see in the dark so the answer is to get some reflective thumb tacks and stick them to the trees along the trail that you wish to take. Remember the mini-mag? The beam of light from the mini mag, flashed down the reflective trail, will light up your path like a highway.

☐ If you want to try rattling to pull a buck out of the woods and if you want to try to harvest him with your bow, it is best to attempt it with two people. A shooter and a rattler. The best times to attempt this is before and after the main rut. The best locations are just outside of feeding and bedding areas. Another good location is near thick cover where you know or suspect that a nice buck would inhabit. When rattling, it is best to pick a location that gives you good cover and also gives you a good field of view and a clear shot. If you are hunting with a firearm it is OK to do this alone or with another who is close. However, if you are hunting with a bow, it is sometimes better to place the hunter in a concealed position between the rattler and the anticipated location where you expect the buck to come in. This method should be used because of the limited range of archery equipment. Remember to use the wind to your advantage.

☐ When rattling you are imitating the sound of two bucks fighting over a hot doe (one that is in estrus or heat). You can use antlers or sheds from deer to imitate this sound. They also have imitation horns which you can use. When banging these horns together you are trying to sound like two bucks fighting. You can also bang and stomp on the ground with your feet and the horns to imitate the sound of hoofs striking the ground while the fight is on.

☐ When hunting deer in the early month of September it is best to find out what food source the deer are using. Armed with this information you can set up an ambush location in a suitable area where the food source is. Because the food source changes as the time goes on they can be eating acorns in one part of the month and then corn, mushrooms, clover etc. in the other part of the month. The trick is to find out what they are eating during the time of year that you wish to harvest them. Why not try this?

If you or a friend harvest a deer, get a good look at the stomach contents. The information gathered from within the deer's stomach cavity will indicate what kind of food that they will be eating at the time. Armed with this information you will know what food source areas would be best to hunt in.

☐ If you wish to have a cheap, easy method to eliminate your scent while you are in the house or in your camp. Why not try this? Place your hunting clothes in a clean scent free plastic garbage bag and sprinkle baking soda on it. Close the bag up over night and in the morning you will have odor free hunting clothes to hunt with.

PRACTICE MAKES PERFECT

19..

☐ Being close to your game means that any sound at all can give away your position. Many times just the noise of your arrow tapping or sliding across your riser or rest can give you away. In order to help conceal this noise, why don't you take a small piece of felt or better yet Dr. Scholl's foot pads and glue it to the inside of your riser. This extra precaution will help deaden the sound of accidentally striking the arrow on the inside face of your riser.

☐ If you want to stop your broadheads from rusting and also from losing some of its edge as it is exposed to the air, after sharpening why not place a light coating of Vaseline on them and they will not be exposed to these conditions.

RAZOR SHARP BROADHEADS ARE A MUST

☐ If you are shooting your bow using shooting gloves you will want to keep your hands as warm as you can especially during the colder months. Wear wool gloves and cut the three shooting fingers out of them and place them over your shooting gloves. This will not affect your shooting ability and will give your hands extra warmth.

☐ After making your hit on the animal it is in your best interest to move as little as possible and to stay quiet. The bow being a silent weapon often causes the animal to stand there or run off a short distance after being hit. Because of the razor sharp broadhead many times the animal does not realize what has happened and will expire without travelling into dirty bush which will make more work for you to pull it out.

☐ If you want to make yourself a bow holder that will easily hold your bow and at the same time allow it to be in accessible reach. Why not build this? Using a piece of 1/4 inch steel, cut out this form to the exact size and shape as this diagram.

Drill a 1/4 inch hole through it and another one through the frame on the side of your metal treestand about eight inches from the end. Dip the U shaped bow holder

HOLE

in liquid rubber and allow it to dry out.

Attach the bow holder to the side of the treestand using a screw and wing nut and place the bottom section of your bow limb in it while you are in the stand The angle that the bow sits at will depend on what location you place your bottom bow limb on.

☐ If you are hunting a species of animal such as a moose from ground level and you know that the animal sees you it is probably assessing you as a potential threat.
If you walk straight towards it the animal will flee and you will not get the opportunity for a shot. Why not try walking in a slow grazing pattern as if wandering with no purpose? By doing this you can slowly angle towards the animal and you will appear as less of a threat. Many times by using this method you will be able to get within bow range and put some meat on the table.

☐ When using scents, be careful that the scent that you use is done so with a little bit of common sense. As an example one does not use apple scent as an attractant food scent in an area where apples do not exist.
There are several different kinds of scents and they usually consist of, cover scents, sex scents, attractant scents and food scents. You do not use the food, sex and attractant scents as a cover scent any more than you would use a sex scent as a food or cover scent.
The right scent has to be used at the right time of the year in the right location and situations.
Many times the misuse of scents has been the downfall of many hunters.   ..22..

☐ If you are hunting scrapes, keep in mind that the location of that scrape was picked because of the location of the overhanging branch which is used by the whitetail buck to leave a secretion from its eye gland. The buck then paws the ground and leaves a single foot print in the scrape as a signature of sorts telling others that he is in the area. Other bucks, if they find the scrape will also use it in the same manner and this causes the buck(s) to become more active in this area. If you find a location such as this and set up a stand, it is very possible for the hunter to shoot several bucks off of the same scrape. As a point of interest. If you accidentally tamper with or break that overhanging branch, the area will no longer be of interest to the bucks and they will no longer come in to it.

Chad Marchand with a Whitetail buck
..23..

☐ If you wish to make a mock scrape for whitetails one has to be very careful with scent. The ideal situation is to find a nearby scrape and or rub line and pick a spot that will be ideal for you to set up a ground blind or preferably a treestand. Make sure that the wind will be blowing from the scrape to you. Using a branch or the tip of your bow, scrape the ground clear of top soil, leaves, branches and any debris which may be on the ground. Make sure that this is done under an overhanging branch which can be anywhere from three feet to five or so feet off the ground. While you are doing this work it is best to wear rubber, doctors surgical gloves as they will not transfer your scent into the area. Now place a bit of scent on the overhanging branch and then place some on a small branch about two inches or so long and place it in the middle of the scrape. Cover the scent on the stick with a leaf and leave it be. It is best to use a scent that is made for this type of use and stuff like Doe urine just doesn't cut it. You need a sex scent.

☐ When tracking a hit animal remember that for every pound the animal weighs it has one ounce of blood. In order for that animal to die it has to lose one third of its blood supply. This blood loss also includes the blood within its body cavity. An example is estimate a deer to weigh 100 pounds. It has 100 ounces of blood. The deer has to lose 33 ounces of blood to fall asleep on its feet from lack of oxygen.   ..24..

☐ When setting up your treestand try to place it within eighteen yards of your shooting area. At this distance you will notice that there is less chance of the animal jumping the string and your chances of a cleaner more humane kill are increased.

SUPPORT YOUR LOCAL AND PROVINCIAL WILDLIFE ORGANIZATIONS

☐ If you are making or buying your arrows it is real nice to think that you should be completely camouflaged right to the arrows. When the arrow companies made the camouflage arrow they hit the jackpot in financial ingenuity. There have been more camouflaged arrows lost and more money spent replacing them than ever before. While I agree that camouflage is necessary, your arrow should be more easy to spot. This makes it easier to determine the location of your hit and arrow recovery. Using an arrow that is autumn orange does not get picked out by the animal and is not taken as a threat by them. I have yet to hear from any experienced bowhunter or arrow producer that the color of the arrow will scare the animal off. On the other hand the color of the fetching on ones arrow if it was white in color could easily be picked out by an animal especially whitetails. They use the white underside of their tail as a signal for danger. Because of this a white flash indicates danger to them.

☐ If you are using your bow for hunting there is one thing that you should keep in mind. The more gadgets and equipment that you put on your bow, the more weight you have to carry and the more things that can go wrong. Remember you are not target shooting now, you are bowhunting and this is a whole different ball game. You are dealing with low light, wind, cold, heavy bush, snow, rain and rougher use of your equipment. It is best to keep your bow as simple and as effective as you deem necessary. Too many times I see archers shooting light bows and arrows with all the bells and whistles on it and come hunting season, use this gear, much of it is not designed for this kind of use.

☐ When setting up your treestand place your steps in about 18 inches apart. The best way to determine this is to screw in a step and place your foot on it. Now with your foot on the step place the other step even with your knee level on the opposite side of the tree. By doing this you can easily walk up the tree without any effort. Once at the desired height make sure that you place the last step in such a manner that it will not interfere with the placing of your treestand. At the same time it will allow you to easily access the stand without getting in the way.

SHARE YOUR GAME WITH LANDOWNERS

☐ Many times the placing of tree steps can be tiring work. As many of the trees are made of hardwoods and often times the trees are frozen. An easy tip is to bring a little battery hand powered drill in with you. Drill the holes in the tree and then screw your tree steps in these holes. This will make your job easier and little effort will be used to put up your stand.

☐ When approaching a downed animal come at it from behind. Look at its eyes. An animal does not die with its eyes closed. If they are closed he is alive. If they are open and you want to see if the animal is expired, touch its eye with the tip of your broadhead. Watch out for horns and hoofs.

☐ Many people think that if you call a moose and it hears you that it will come charging out. This is usually not the case. A cow call is used to tell the bull that she is in the area. Many times a bull will stick around the area of the calling and will not come in for one reason or another. Sometimes when giving a bull call, the bull that hears the call may be a small one and is intimidated into thinking that a bigger bull is in the area and he will get his butt kicked. Many times it is necessary to work an area for several days and I think that this is best to do with a cow call. Once a bull moose shows interest then you can get him in closer by grunting like a bull. Make him think that there is a little competition in the area trying to get there ahead of him. If the bull starts grunting in response to your calls and you really want to get him upset just repeat every call that he makes. This action gets their dander up and when he comes in he might make that big mistake.

Rick Marchand with his bow harvested Ontario Moose

☐ If you want to know what kind of head gear the deer has that is working on the scrape that you are hunting, take a look at the branches that are above the over hanging branch above the scrape. If these branches appear broken or have marks on the bark they are usually made by the antlers of the deer while they are rubbing their eye glands on the over hanging branch. This usually indicates that the buck working the scrape is a good one and worthwhile hunting. Deep gouges made in trees on rubs will also indicate a big antlered buck.

☐ When stalking bears on the ground, try to stalk the animal downwind and come in from behind it or on its left side. Black bears are predominantly left handed and because of this, their left hand is doing the most work. With this is mind, that arm will be moving more often rooting grubs etc. and obstructing its vision more often. This gives you an extra edge to get closer for that good bow shot.
This habit also causes them to run more often to the right when startled. The reason for this is that they know that they have not seen danger come in from that direction. Armed with this information you can anticipate that there will be a higher percentage chance for a shot knowing that it will turn right to run off.

Caribou are easy animals to get close to and harvest with a bow and arrow. The trick with these animals is to hunt the migratory trails which they use every year. Find a good place to set up an ambush along their trails and wait for them. Eventually they will come along and a well placed arrow will knock them down.

The Author with a Quebec Labrador Caribou
..30..

☐ If you are hunting cougar with your bow try to find a recent deer kill that they are working on. Cougar will kill about one deer a week and will stay with it till it's gone. The mountain lions are very short breathed and if they are feeding on a kill and are chased off of it with dogs, they usually will tree in a very short distance.

This Pope & Young cougar taken by the author in B.C.

◻ Going duck and goose hunting with a bow and arrow can also be a great way to get out of cleaning ducks and geese. However there are many bowhunters who can do it. Here is one word of warning which can happen to you so be careful. It would be best not to use your labrador retriever to fetch these birds as many times the arrow will stay in the bird and when the dog is bringing the bird in, it is very easy for the dog to get stabbed by the arrow in the bird leading to a dead or injured dog and a vet bill.

◻ In order to prevent the deer that you are shooting at from jumping the string, try to set up your shot so that it is from either eighteen yards or less or thirty two yards or more. Studies have shown that these distances have the best chances of the animals either not being able to react to the shot or not hear it coming. Shots over forty yards should not be attempted.

WHITETAIL DEER CAN JUMP A STRING AND DROP A FULL BODY LENGTH IN TWO TO THREE TENTHS PER SECOND

◻ Bowhunting from a canoe can be very productive. Try placing foam pipe insulation over the gunnels on both sides of the canoe in front of you. In this way you can lay your bow and paddle across the width of the canoe. It will protect your bow and will also reduce the noise of you removing the bow to make that shot. Caution, watch out for your lower limb when shooting.

☐ When purchasing your broadheads consider buying one that start cutting on impact. Heads that have cone shaped or chisel shaped points lose a lot of their penetrating power as they have to open the hide with a hole before the blades start to cut. In doing this a lot of energy is expended from the arrows impact and lessens the possibility of better penetration.

☐ If you do use fixed broadheads (ones that have to be sharpened) consider sharpening the back blades on the heads as well. The more cutting surface that you have that comes in contact with veins, muscles, arteries etc, the better your chances are to humanly harvest your animal.

RESPECT LAND OWNERS RIGHTS

☐ When looking for a good location to ambush your prey, especially whitetails, look for funnel areas. By this I mean, areas that form a natural funnel type of cover which allows the animal to move from one area to another with the least likely chance of being seen. This can be a growth of trees between two fields or bedding and feeding areas.

There can be many different variables that bring about a funnel area. As an example I have one favorite spot that has a steep hill going down behind me and about fifty feet of bush then an old road in front of me. On the other side of the road is a steep hill going up. The animals are not very keen to walk along the roadway and expose themselves so they utilize this fifty feet of wood for cover. If you wish to pick out funnel areas in your hunting spot easily, try looking at aerial photographs of the location or find a pilot that likes to fly and offer to pay his gas. These funnel areas will just jump right up at you once you know what to look for.

☐ If you are not into treestands and wish to set up a blind area you might as well make yourself comfortable. Find a sitting spot downwind from your ambush spot yet close enough to allow an easy hit. Use some branches to allow you some cover and get some camouflage netting that is compatible with the surrounding area. Set it up around you and sit your rear end down on a small Camouflage stool or chair. Make sure that the area around your feet is clear of branches, leaves and other such debris so that when you stand up to shoot there will be no noise

**USE THE WIND TO YOUR ADVANTAGE
WHEN HUNTING CLOSE**

☐ When pulling an arrow out of your harvested animal make sure that all the blades are attached to your broadhead. If one is left inside it can easily cut you or the butcher causing unnecessary pain and possibly death to a human being.

☐ If you want a camouflage that will be used as a general purpose use in your treestand why not think of using white skyline camouflage or white coveralls. As surprising as this may seem the color white is not taken as a threat to animals of prey when it is in the air in a tree. I think that when animals look up and see the color white they assume that it is simply white fluffy clouds and they tend to disregard it. A good example of this is in the province of Saskatchewan a hunter must wear solid white or solid orange. When hunters wear the white while sitting in the treestand it has no major effect on the hunting success.

☐ Many hunters would like to get as much penetration from their arrows as possible. With this in mind one thing that I, as well as several other bowhunters have done is to apply a light coating of floor wax to your arrows and rub it in till you get a smooth coating all the way down it. Although the shafts are already very smooth, this extra work will probably assist in your penetration. There is however a down side to this and that is that if you practice with this coating of wax on your arrows in ten test butts the arrows will impact it at a speed which heats up the arrow as it enters the ten test. When this happens the wax will melt on the shaft and then cool down making the ten test stick to your arrow when you pull it out. When this happens it is difficult to remove from the butt and your arrow will have to be washed down with acetone to clean it off.

☐ Many hunters have difficulty sharpening their broadheads. If you use broadheads with replaceable blades this although costly is easy to do simply by buying new ones. If however you are using fixed blades which are usually tougher steel and that you have to sharpen yourself they can be easily sharpened by using a wet stone wheel (see gift suggestions in back of this book). The file and leather strap is a good way to sharpen them however takes a lot of time. I have found that using a wet stone wheel you can put a razor sharp edge on your broadheads with little effort and in no time at all.

☐ This may sound a little stupid but think about this for a minute. Have you ever sat or stood in the bush and thought that you have heard something but were not sure. You listen intently with your mouth open and it seems to help you hear better? All of a sudden out of the blue comes an involuntary cough and you chase off any animal that you may have heard. The problem is that you have stood there with your mouth open and as a result the inside of your mouth gets suddenly dry forcing a cough. When you think you hear something, listen as intently as possible and close your mouth occasionally to allow the moisture to remain. This will suppress that cough and you won't scare anything and reveal your position.

☐ Although I personally think that there are just too many useless accessories that one can put on ones bow. There is one item which I believe is invaluable when you are bowhunting.
This item is known as an arrow holder, Sta Jack or Quick Loc. This little piece of rubber is attached to your bow on the riser or the outside of your sight window. It folds inward and is used to hold your arrow securely in place on the arrow rest while you are waiting for your game to come in. It is especially helpful when sitting in your treestand as the arrow is ready to fire and all you have to do is pull back on your string. This allows you to use as little movement as possible, a big plus when one should keep the movement to a minimum. The device should not be used to keep the arrow on the string while you are walking as this is very unsafe.

☐ If you are using feathers on your hunting arrows and are not happy because of their condition after being exposed to rain and snow. Try spraying them with silicone, the same type that you would use to waterproof your boots. If you do not want to spray them try placing baby bottle liners over your arrows covering your feathers and they will remain dry and protected from the elements. Just poke the nock through the bottom of the bottle liner to hold them on. They can easily be removed once that shot is needed.

☐ If your whitetail deer season goes on later in the year when there is snow on the ground. Simply set up your treestand down wind from a well established deer trail and simply wait. Whitetails are notorious for using the same trails for traveling and they are bound to walk within bow range at anytime of the day. Mornings and evening however are your best bet.

☐ If you are bow hunting bears there is a good chance that it will be in the spring. This is the worst time of the year for flies and they can and will drive you out of your mind. If you are wearing coveralls tape your shirt and pant cuffs with duct tape and wear a head net to ward them off. Gloves with fly dope on them will help to keep them off of your hands. If you so desire it would be best to take one vitamin B 1 pill a day for a week before and during the time that you are hunting in the bush. This will emit a smell from you which repels the pests.

☐ It can be pretty easy to accidentally cut or break your bowstring in the field and this could easily be the end of your hunt. Why not tape an extra bowstring to your bow quiver and make sure that there is a nocking point on it already set in the right position.

☐ When taking aim at any animal bow the best effective location to place your arrow is in the chest lung area. This shot should be taken when the animal is broadside or quartering away. This shot will humanely harvest your animals ensuring a clean quick kill.
Head on and rear end shots should be avoided at all costs.

☐ Have you ever heard about and wondered where some of the glands are on a whitetail buck? Here they are:

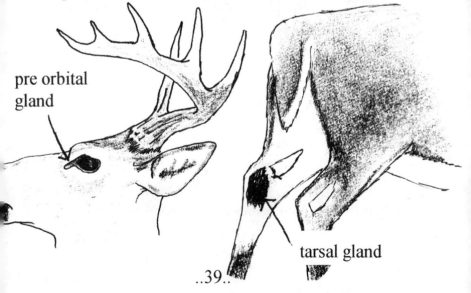

pre orbital gland

tarsal gland

The Glands Of A Whitetail And Their Purposes

☐ Tarsal Gland: This gland is located on the back hocks of the whitetail deer. When in rut the whitetail buck purposely urinates down its legs allowing the urine to saturate the Tarsal glands and this mixes with the secretions of those tarsal glands. This mixture produces a scent to other deer that identifies the particular animal which is making the scent. Many times this action takes place on the scrape that the whitetail buck is working on and identifies that scrape as his. The urine, secretion combination produces a musky smell which hunters sometimes think taints the meat. This is not the case.

☐ Pre orbital Gland: This gland is located in the dark hollow section in the front of the deer's eyes. There is a wax like secretion there that identifies the buck by its individual odor. The whitetail buck will find an overhanging branch from a tree and make a scrape under it. He will then rub the hollow section of its eye into this branch and the odor left on it is a form of signature identifying that particular buck. If you find broken branches above the overhanging branches this is caused by its antlers breaking them while it is rubbing its eyes and this indicates that the buck is a good one.

☐ When pulling back on your bow concentrate on the right spot to place that arrow. As concentration is the key word here, a bowhunter must remember to ignore small distractions before he releases. One mistake that hunters make is that they are so concerned by the size of the animals antlers that their eyes shift to the head of the animal. This shifts the concentration point of the shooter and sometimes results in a less than favorable hit. Keep your eyes off of the head gear and concentrate on that perfect spot.

☐ Many hunters would rather sit at home or in the comfort of their hunting camp when it is raining or snowing outside. Believe it or not but this is the best time to go out in pursuit of your prey. The moisture in the air from rain and snow drives your human odor down into the ground and in doing so prevents the animal from smelling you. If you have a stand location where scent currents are critical this would be a good time to sit in it.

☐ If you are fortunate enough to find a good location for your treestand and have a variety of trees to choose from to place your treestand in. Try to pick a tree that does not produce much sap. Trees like cedars, tamarack and spruce will offer you good cover and has less sticky substance. These trees will not produce as much sap as say, a balsam.

☐ When it comes to sap, this stuff can really make a mess of your screw in tree steps. To remove this sticky substance, try boiling them in an old pot with water. The sap will remove itself from the steps and be as good as new.

☐ There are several different simple ways to help you determine which way the wind is blowing. One is to simply tie a small feather to a string and attach it to your bow tip. A thread can do the same job. Many people like to light up their lighter and look at the direction the flame is going in. A spray bottle filled with baking soda sprayed into the air has the same effect. These methods are good but with wind changes you may have to do this several times and it can prove to be a pain in the butt. The best all around approach is probably your wind feather.

☐ If your string serving is coming undone and you do not want to or cannot change the string, why not simply get a tube of crazy glue and place it on the serving after you have tightened it back up. Some people put the glue on the string whether it is needed or not.

☐ Sometimes it is extremely difficult to get that buck to come close to you for that one good shot. If you are rattling, setting up on a trail or just sitting near a scrape try this. Use a deer decoy to entice him in closer. The decoy will make the deer more relaxed and at the same time it will take the bucks attention away from your area. It is sometimes a good idea to use a grunt tube to get the deer's attention. Place some deer sex scent on the back of the decoy so that if the buck goes downwind of it, it will get a whiff of the deer scent and this will relax him a bit more. You can also put horns on the decoy and if the buck is in rut it may try to chase the buck decoy off, even attack it. Make sure that the decoy is well within your effective shooting distance. You never really know what to expect when using it.   ..43..

☐ If you are using a doe decoy around a deer bait it would be best to take it out with you when you leave. Does have been known to kick the hell out of them in an effort to chase it out of the bait pile. Bucks have been known to viciously attack a buck decoy and destroy it as well.

☐ Care should be taken carrying a decoy into your hunting area. If possible, bring it in unassembled and tie bright colored flagging tape to it while you have it in your possession. Try to set it up in a location that will be unseen by gun hunters so that they will not take pot shots at it.

☐ When removing your arrow with the broadhead from your harvested animal take care not to pull the arrow out while using your other hand to hold down the animal with your fingers around the arrow hole. By doing this you can seriously cut yourself as the arrow is removed and this can really screw up a good trip.

☐ Although many provinces and states have hunting bow weight minimums of 35 to 45 pounds for legal hunting. You should consider using a bow with at least 55 pounds for hunting big game animals.

☐ If you want to go the route of face camouflage and want to paint yourself up, here are some of the things to watch out for. The shine from your face is more prominent in certain areas and it is these spots that you make sure that you pay attention to.
The shiney spots which are easily picked out are: cheek bones, ears, forehead, chin, under the eyes, the neck and your hands.

☐ When going moose or elk hunting it is extremely effective to call the animal as you are slowly walking into your ambush location. In doing this you are covering more area while you are walking in and at the same time you have a better opportunity to get the animal to follow your call to your ambush location.
It is not advisable to try this method using a predator call while you are walking in thick bush in Grizzly country.

UTILIZE ALL OF YOUR HARVESTED ANIMAL

☐ While bowhunting moose and looking for an area where they might live, try looking for areas where there is an abundance of beavers. The combination of food source and water that is appealing to beavers is the same combination that the moose require. Once this kind of location is found you can locate a good game trail, Set up a downwind ambush area and call them in.

Rick Marchand with his Northern Ontario moose
..46..

☐ If you harvest an animal with your archery equipment do not exhibit or display the animal in a picture with the arrow in it. This leaves a bad taste in everyone's mouth and does not show the respect that the animal deserves. When taking the picture make sure that the tongue is in the mouth and that the blood has been wiped away. Do not display the head on your vehicle or lay the body on the hood of your vehicle displayed to the public. It is this kind of action that the animal rights fanatics crave and use against hunters.

WHEN BOWHUNTING, USE THE WIND TO YOUR ADVANTAGE

☐ Many times we have heard that a buck in rut is not suitable to eat and that there is a strong odor to it. The meat IS excellent table fare and this is an old wives tale that needs to be dispelled. The thick musky odor that one smells when you approach a downed animal in rut comes from its tarsal glands which are located on the hocks of its rear legs. The deer urinates down its legs and the urine runs into and down its tarsal glands. This produces the musky odor which makes the smell so prominent. Some hunters believe that if they smell this odor, the meat is inedible. This is not true. the meat is not tainted by this effect.

☐ If you are looking for an area that has everything that big game requires, try looking for locations that are abundant in small game animals. Once this area is located you can be assured that there is ample food and cover which are used by the big game animals as well.

☐ If you have harvested an animal and you or a friend wish to continue to hunt in that area, it is advisable to drag the body off into another location to clean it. This is sometimes not possible with animals such as moose or elk. The reason for this is that predators will be attracted to the area by the gut pile. Once the bears, coyotes and wolves are in there they will eat the remains of the animal and will probably kill another one in that same area. Pretty soon the region is filled with predators which in turn will kill or chase the game away this location. If you are hunting where there is a multiple deer limit as an example, it is best to bag the internal organs of the deer in a plastic bag or clean it somewhere else.

..48..

LETS LOOK INSIDE

☐ Many times when you have hit an animal you wonder just what organs or vitals your arrow has struck. There are many variables that have to be considered and the purpose of these diagrams is to help you make a rational decision as to what your next move should be. Always keep in mind the bow is a silent weapon and once the animal is hit you should keep as quiet as possible to stop the animal from fleeing out of fright.

In the next three diagrams of moose, deer and bear I will attempt to show you what to look out for and where your best percentage shots should be taken to make a clean humane kill.

The moose: There is a common misconception among some hunters that the hump of the moose is the place to aim. The hump consists of muscle and meat. It is also the place that contains the spine. Many old timers tell us to aim for the hump. This is not a humane shot and is not the brightest thing to do. The reason that you hear this is because occasionally the bullet (not arrow) will break the spine when the animal is hit there. This causes the animal to drop instantly and requires another shot to finish it off. That is because of the shock, impact effect of a bullet. An arrow does not have this. This type of shot with a firearm is also responsible for many wounded animals.

☐ The best location to place a shot with a bow or a firearm is the heart, lung region. This gives you the highest percentage most humane kill available. If you hit the animal in the lungs, the blood on the ground or on your arrow will be frothy. There is a vein called the aorta. This vein is located high on the heart and is the main artery connected to it. If this is hit the animal will die in seconds. The blood supply to the brain will be cut off and it will be unconscious almost immediately. Blood from this region is dark red.

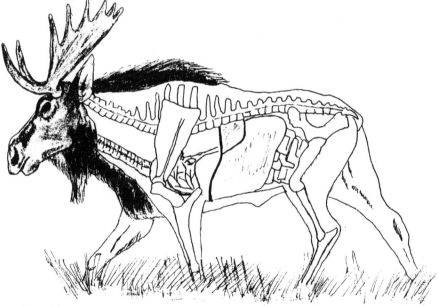

There is a bone that is connected to the shoulder blade to the elbow of the moose. This bone is called a humerus and is not a funny bone. When the moose is moving this bone partially covers the heart, lung area and you should be careful to shoot when the leg is forward in order to give you a higher percentage shot.

If you hit the animal in the lungs you will notice that the blood on your arrow will be frothy. It is considered a easier shot on the heart, lung area with a bow when the animal is quartering away slightly. The arrow will have less obstruction if it slides in behind the ribs into the chest cavity. In this way there are no ribs to slow down or obstruct the arrow.

There are several arteries and veins on the animal which are only about the thickness of a pencil. These are the femoral artery and the arterial arteries. When a arrow cuts through these, the animal is usually done like dinner. However this shot should not be purposely tried as the target area is just to small.

☐ Head on shots on all animals should never be attempted, especially on a moose. Where the top of the ribs meet the bottom of the neck there is a opening about the size of a mans fist. If this region was hit it would mean a killing shot. This however, is a totally uncalled for shot to take as there are just to many variables that come into play. First, the target is too small. Second, the arrow can easily deflect off of the ribs wounding the animal. Thirdly, the head and nose of the moose are very long and large . A moose has but to lower it's head a few inches and this spot is completely covered. The result is that the moose will probably get a shot in the beak.

☐ Rear shots or Texas heart shots as they are sometimes called can also occasionally be a fatal hit. The arrow will, if placed properly enter the soft under belly from behind and enter the heart, lung region. This is an extremely low percentage shot and should not be tried. This shot causes the meat to have a sour taste as the arrow must penetrate through the stomach pouch cutting open the guts etc. This is unsatisfactory and should not be attempted.

The black bear: Again broadside shots and quartering away shots should be taken in the heart, lung region of the animal to insure a quick clean humane kill.

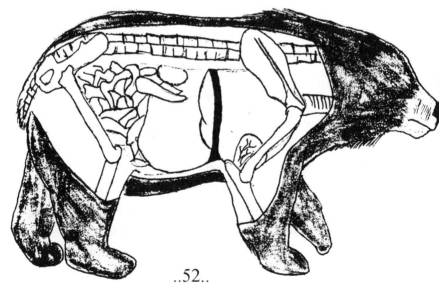

The bear has a huge plate like shoulder blade which actually acts as a shield over the front upper region of its heart, lung area. When the bear is below you, say you are shooting from a tree stand or from the side of a hill or mountain, you must keep this in mind. These two shoulder blades cover up a good chunk of the kill zone. In order to have the optimum opportunity to harvest your bear try shooting at it when the leg facing you is forward giving you a more unobstructed shot.

With a bow, head on shots on bears should never be tried unless the bear is standing up and facing you.

☐ A bears hide is usually very loose and in the fall it is a very fat animal. For this reason the entrance and exit hole on the bear can be clogged up with the fat and close up because of the loose hide going over the wound. This slows down and prevents the blood flow from exiting the animal. This in turn leaves a poor exit trail. While I realize that this is a bowhunting tip book, if a wounded or fatally hit bear goes into extremely thick bush and stays there it usually makes a bow shot impossible. You must go after it. It would be wise to take a in firearm with you. You need a weapon that is short and fast for close range and that packs a wallop to stop it in its tracks. I would suggest a pump riot gun 12 gauge with 3" magnum shells with hollow point slugs or SSG. In cases like this it is not time to fool around. Keep in mind however that if you wish to enter your bear in the Pope & Young books, they will not accept it if it has been shot with a firearm.

The whitetail deer: This animal is one which runs on pure adrenaline. Once hit, the deer when spooked can run quite a distance before collapsing. It is for this reason that a bowhunter should make as little movement or sound as possible during and after the shot. The frame work of the deer is similar to the moose with the exception of the large humerus bone and the hump on its back.

▢ Whitetail deer have several habits that are noticeable characteristics when they are hit. Usually when hit the deer will run with its tail down. This indicates to you that a hit has been made. Many times when they are hit they will circle around to go back in the same direction that they had come from.
Often times when they are hit in the liver or kidneys, they will run away with their back hunched up.

▢ Because a whitetail deer is such a high strung animal and all of its senses are so acute (as compared to not so cute). If you have the opportunity to see one coming towards you, it would be wise to let him pass by you. This is so that it will give you a good quartering away shot. In this way you will have a better opportunity to harvest him as he will be more attuned to the area that he is walking towards then where he has just been. The deer will have a false sense of security behind it as no danger had been encountered there while it passed by you.

☐ Bowhunting turkeys with a bow is extremely hard because of the movement that a bowhunter must make in drawing back the bow. This compounded with the fact that the turkey has extremely sharp eyesight makes it a real challenge. To help beat these odds, try hunting them with two hunters. One calls and the other is the shooter about forty or so yards away. Place a turkey decoy between them. Let the turkey walk between the hunter and the caller. When the turkey has walked past the hunter let him shoot it from behind as its attention is focused on the decoy and the caller.

GIVE YOUR SURPLUS MEAT TO THE NEEDY LET THEM KNOW THAT YOU ARE A BOWHUNTER

☐ In bowhunting every animal that you take should be considered as a trophy. The skills needed to get close enough to harvest the animal on its own terms demands it. There is no shame in harvesting a doe as an example. The term "Trophy Hunting" is not one that I approve of. It implies that the animal is harvested because of its head gear or skull size and that the animal is not utilized. This leaves a bad taste in everybody's mouth and helps to fuel the fires of hate within the animals rights fanatics that are out there. If you wish to hold out for such an animal well so be it. That is your choice. Just don't use the term trophy hunting and utilize all of the animal. When the public was interviewed in many polls. One of the biggest concerns that where expressed, was that they opposed the harvesting of animals just for the trophy. Don't let yourself fall into this category.

If you want to try your hand at bowfishing, you will need to get yourself a bowfishing kit. The reel is screwed into or taped to your riser on your bow. You must get yourself a good set of polarized sunglasses to help you see the fish in the water. They also help to cut down the glare. When aiming at the fish, aim lower than the fish actually appears at. The combination of sunlight and water refraction plays tricks on you in determining the actual depth of the water.

☐ During the bow hunting season a hunter should refrain from walking along deer trails. This method can and will interfere with other hunters who may be on stands or blinds. The walking along these trails leaves a scent trail along it which will stop the deer from using it until the scent is gone.

☐ If you do decide to walk along deer trails or through the woods in a stalking method, remember the wind thermal's. In the morning stalk downhill and in the evening stalk uphill. If you do not do this the thermal's will carry your scent ahead of you and this in turn will alert the game that you are hunting of your arrival way before you get to them.

☐ It is important to get to your hunting location before daylight. At least one hour before. This is so that the scent that you have left on your way in will dissipate by time the shooting light comes in and this will give you an extra edge.

☐ If you are hunting on land that has fences on it. Consider spending extra time hunting where the fence meets up with another or angles at a 90 degree bend. Wildlife like cattle will follow a fence line and many times will cross where the fences meet.

CHAPTER TWO
Treestand Hunting Tips

TREESTAND TIPS

☐ After setting up your treestand for whatever species that you wish to harvest, many hunters take it for granted that there is nothing left to do but wait. They will sit there waiting for their prey to come in and when it does they will lean forward in their stand or stand up to shoot only to find out that the noise of their clothes pulling away from the trunk of the tree sounds like a Velcro commercial. How to overcome this?

One easy method is to scrape the bark off of the tree in the location where you will be leaning against. This method however does not always work.

Another simple method is to go to your local carpet shop and ask them for some of their out of stock carpet samples. These are about two feet square and they will usually give them away. Find some that have a color that is fairly compatible with the surroundings that you are hunting in and bring them to your treestand. Nail or staple these samples to the trunk of the tree where you will come in contact with it. This should silence any noise your clothes would make should it rub against the tree. Sometimes there will be frozen dirt or ice particles and snow stuck to your boots. This causes a crunching noise as you step on the base of your treestand. The crunching noise can also be eliminated by laying the carpet samples on the base of the treestand.

☐ If you are going to use a pull up rope on your treestand to pull up your bow and equipment try to get one that is green or a dark color so that it blends in with the tree. Making it difficult to spot.

☐ If you want to set up your treestand along game trails and you are not sure what area to do this in, try this. Place your stand downwind from the trail in an location that has a curve in it or an intersection with other trails. Make sure that it is within your effective shooting range. Animals will walk slower in these areas to check out the trails ahead of them thus giving you a better chance at getting a good shot as they will be looking down these trails to make sure that it is safe to go on.

RESPECT LANDOWNERS RIGHTS

☐ Many times I have been asked by hunters what to do if you are in your treestand and there is a bear or deer under it that you do not want to harvest and you do not want to give away your location. It is getting dark and you do not relish the thought of having to walk out at night or spending the night in the tree. Take your hat or your glove and throw it in the direction of the animal without drawing attention to yourself. The scent of human odor from the article of clothing usually makes them back away from that location without really spooking them too much. If that does not work you can either spend the rest of the night up the tree or you can have a previous understanding with a partner that he walks in to check up on you. This will scare the animals off, not give away your position and you can safely come down.

☐ When placing your treestand, try to put it in a location that is well shaded and that offers you a good amount of cover to help conceal you. If there is none, consider tying branches under, behind and over the treestand in the supporting tree.

☐ Many people including myself occasionally like to paint a stand before the hunting season. This prevents the stand from rusting and also provides a sort of camo color which helps to hide the stand. If you do decide to do this, paint it in the winter months after the hunting season. In this way the smell of paint will be gone by the time the hunting season comes and the smell will not alarm the animals. Primer rust proof paint is probably the best

SAFETY FIRST, USE YOUR SAFETY BELT

☐ Every hunter when in his or her stand must keep safety in mind. Always use a safety belt tied to a tree and yourself. You can use a commercially bought one, old seat belt or if necessary a rope and leave about twelve to eighteen inches of line between the tree and yourself.

.

☐ Once your treestand is set up and secure move your bow arm into different shooting positions while on the stand. By doing this you can determine if there are any branches or obstructions that may be in your way while you are shooting. A saw placed at the end of a broom handle or a tree pruner can be used to cut the branches which are out of your reach and may affect the flight of your arrow.

☐ Screwing in a tree step or cutting a branch about four inches from the tree trunk above you will allow you a place to hang your fanny pack or pack sack within easy reaching distance. Make sure that it is not placed in a location that will interfere with your head or shoulders when you stand up. If you are worried that someone will come along and steal your treestand while you are gone, try chaining it to a tree and lock it there with a key type lock. On your descent take out the last five steps and hide them near the stand or take them out with you.

☐ When setting up your treestand another thing that you have to watch out for is ground shadows. A well placed and concealed treestand can be totally ruined if your shadow is cast over the trail or spot that you expect the animal to come in on. Try to make sure that the suns position will not go against you so that when you move to shoot, the shadow movement will be detected on the ground by the animal.

☐ In many provinces and states such as Ontario and Michigan it is illegal to build a permanent treestand in a tree. However in areas where it is legal and these stands are allowed it can be a real hummer to sit there for many hours in the cold weather. If this is the case why not try this?
Close in some of the wall areas on the stand and haul up a small propane tank with a propane heater attachment connected to it. You can light it up and it will keep you warm while you are waiting for the animal to come along. The hissing noise of the burning propane in the heater does not affect the game and there seems to be no smell which will give your position away.

☐ Many bowhunters who have been hunting in the same stand in the evening and the morning will leave their bow in the stand overnight. In this way they do not have to carry it in or out and depending on the law they do not have to encase it. This is not a very good idea. If there are porcupines in the area they will often climb trees and chew on the riser on your bow, damaging it. The salt from the sweat on our hands soaks into the wooden risers and the porcupines are attracted to it and they will chew on it.

FAMILY, BOWHUNTING AND NATURE A BEAUTIFUL COMBINATION

☐ One thing to keep in mind when tracking a hit animal is that often animals which are seriously hit have more of a tendency to travel downhill than up. You can use this to your advantage when you lose its trail.

☐ When waiting in your treestand for game to come along, it can be a real pain when your presence is discovered by squirrels. They love to chatter up a storm and in doing so they let every animal in the area know that you are there.
Why not use these animals to your advantage?
Once you have set up your tree stand. Sit very still and don't give them a reason to make any noise about you. Instead watch them. You will find that when

an animal comes close to you the
little rodent will stop everything
and stare in the direction that the
animal is coming in. He will then
take off in double time and this will
be your cue to get ready as chances

are pretty good that something is coming towards you. I
have one friend who claims that while in his stand he
always carries a handful of peanuts and he throws them
down one or two at a time towards the squirrels. This
feeds them and keeps them quiet. When a bear comes in
to his bait he is alerted by the actions of his squirrel.

WHY NOT MAKE ARCHERY AND
BOWHUNTING A FAMILY AFFAIR?

☐ When hunting from a treestand you should have several
different locations available with stands in them. The
longer that you stay in one position the less chance that
you have to harvest an animal from that stand. Eventually
the excess of human odor will overwhelm that location.

☐ Several times in your hunting career you will find a
great stand location but can only use it when the wind is
blowing in a certain direction. This can be maddening
when you know that this is a hot area. When you come
across this, why not place two tree stands up, one on each

side of the location so that you can use one stand when the wind is favoring it and one stand when the wind favors the other one.

☐ Bears can be very sneaky and smart especially when you come across a big one. These animals will usually lay down just outside of a perimeter around your treestand and bait and they will wait till you leave. They will usually come in downwind of your stand once you are gone.
There are several ways to try to trick him. One is to bring in an old sweaty T-shirt with your odor on it and leave it at the bait site all the time that you are baiting it. This will get the bear used to your odor and he sometimes will not know if he can smell you there or not.
Another thing to do in this instance is to walk in to the bait pile with a friend and once you are settled down in your treestand have the friend walk out. The bear, thinking that you have left will feel more confident coming in, giving you a better chance for a shot.

☐ On a bait that has bears hitting it why not try this? Every time you leave the area after baiting it, beep the horn of your truck. If this is impossible try making some other kind of distinctive noise that is loud enough to be heard by the bears. Leave a hunter in the stand and then walk out making the noise as you leave. To the bears this will be like a dinner bell. If there are multiple bears on the bait do not take the first one that comes in. Bears have a pecking order and they work around it. Usually if you hear a bear that comes in to the bait woofing, this is in order to let the other bears know that he is coming in and for them to clear out. This usually indicates that this is the dominant bear on that bait.

The author with a P&Y black bear
..69..

If you want to position a whitetail deer and get him to come to you from trails that are running nearby here's how you do it. Get an old fly fishing reel that has some dry line on it. Using rubber gloves place some gel type sex lure scent on the line. Lay the line along the ground making sure that the line crosses deer trails that you would suspect the deer to travel on. The line can also be laid from a scrape as well. Lay the line along the ground past your treestand location and well within an accurate shooting distance for your bow. When your buck comes along and crosses this scent line you will notice that it will walk from one end of the line to the other looking for the doe at the end of the trail. This will give you several opportunities to take a shot at the wandering buck as its nose will probably be down towards the ground trying to pick up the scent. When you leave the area remember to reel in the fishing line again using the rubber gloves.

☐ When lowering your bow, do so in such a manner that your bow is placed on the ground where it will not interfere with your descent from the tree. You do not want to step on it accidentally breaking it or your arrows.

☐ Once your hunt is over and it is time to take it down your stand. Lower your bow with the pull up rope. DO NOT take down the stand and let it drop to the ground with the bow still attached to the pull up rope. If you do drop the treestand the rope may hook on a branch or tree step and while the stand is going down the bow will be going up possibly destroying your bow and equipment.

☐ If you are uncertain about how high you are when setting up your treestand, why not try this.
Measure out a length of rope to the distance that you wish to place your stand in the tree from the ground. Tie one end of the rope to the stand which will be laying on the ground. As you climb the tree, take the rope up with you. When you run out of rope, you will know that you have reached the desired height. You can now use this rope to pull the treestand up and secure it to the tree. You can now use this rope as your pull up rope.

☐ If you are looking for a treestand to purchase, consider buying one that has a high seat. You will be spending many hours in it and if your seat is low, your legs will easily begin to feel cramped, sore and fall asleep. The best treestand that I have found to date that fits this bill is the screaming eagle treestand. I will mentioned this stand later on in this book under Gifts For The Bowhunter.

☐ Wind currents can sometimes play havoc on you even when you are at different heights in your treestand. Before the hunting season if you want to see which way the currents are blowing from the treestand location that you wish to hunt in, why not try this. Place your treestand up and stay up there. Have another person on the ground and from your treestand release a smoke grenade or smoke bomb. The smoke will easily show you where the wind currents are going and armed with this information you will know where your scent will be going. I would suggest that you try this in the mornings and evenings.

**SAFETY FIRST, ALWAYS WEAR
YOUR SAFETY BELT.
ITS NOT THE FALL THAT KILLS YOU
IT'S THE SUDDEN STOP**
..73..

CHAPTER THREE
Bowhunting Answers

BOWHUNTING ANSWERS

There are many people out there who are ignorant of the many aspects of bowhunting. This section is to help you, the bowhunter, to better explain to them the principles behind it and in turn help to educate the non hunting public. Communication is necessary to better make these people understand.

☐ Bowhunting is a very humane method of harvesting animals. The arrow heads are razor sharp and can cause little or no pain. When a doctor operates, he uses a razor sharp scalpel. This is because the cut he makes is easier to heal and less painful. When a man or woman cuts themselves shaving, many times they are not aware of it until they see the blood on the face cloth or in the mirror. This is because of the razor sharpness of the blade. I have seen and shot animals where the sharp broadhead passed right through them and they continue to eat. Not knowing what has happened.

☐ Bullets kill by impact and shock. Arrows kill by hemorrhaging or bleeding to death. An animal struck by an arrow will bleed either externally or internally or both. This blood loss results in a lack of oxygen within its system which in turn makes the animal tired and it will literally fall asleep on its feet. This is a painless and humane process. A razor sharp broadhead will have the same effect as a scalpel. Ask any doctor.

ONE MUST UNDERSTAND THAT HUNTING IN ANY FORM IS A CULTURAL, SOCIAL AND SPIRITUAL HERITAGE FOR THE HUNTER AND THE COMMUNITY

☐ Often, we as bowhunters, will hear that people believe that there are too many wounded deer out there caused by bowhunters. This is not the case. What usually causes this is the fact that occasionally an animal is seen with an arrow protruding out of its body. It is because the arrow is visible and as such it is more noticeable. Unfortunately, this does happen occasionally. What is not taken into consideration is that this wound, although obvious, will probably heal quickly and the chances of that animal's survival are considerably high. Again that is because of the scalpel like sharpness of the broadhead. Sharp cuts heal faster remember. An arrowhead that has entered an animal and stays in the meat usually is surrounded by a callus. This callus acts as a protective barrier around the object and the animal is no worse for wear. Arrow hit animals have a far higher survival rate than other injuries received.

BOWHUNTER EDUCATION, THE WAY TO GO

☐ A bow is a close quarters weapon. Unfortunately we have a lot of hunters entering the bowhunting seasons with little bow hunting experience. Because of this we notice that there are shots taken at longer distances and with less than adequate equipment. Many of these are gun hunters who do not realize the limitations of the bow as a weapon and continually are thinking like gun hunters instead of bow hunters. Education is the only real answer and the governments must soon realize that this is necessary. If you see anyone in the woods who falls into this category try to make them understand what they are doing wrong and suggest that they enter into an International Bowhunter Education Program.

☐ Bowhunting is not for everybody. If your intention is to fill your freezer consistently while using your bow and arrow. Forget it. You are best to use a firearm.
Bowhunting is for the person who appreciates and enjoys the beauty of the outdoors and in doing so becomes one with and a part of the nature around him. If while using

the bow during this oneness, we harvest an animal on its own terms and in its own environment then that is a plus. One should learn to appreciate nature and try to become part of it. That is what bowhunting is about.

THE BEST WAY TO ENSURE HUNTING'S FUTURE IS TO SHARE YOUR KNOWLEDGE AND HUNTING GROUNDS WITH YOUNG HUNTERS

☐ If you do want to be fairly successful you must use the bow as often as possible. A sincere bowhunter will have his bow with him whenever possible and leave the guns at home. You will be surprised at how often the right opportunity will come along all of a sudden and you will be in the right place at the right time. Think back to some of the animals that you have harvested during your gun hunting days. Think of how many were close enough to take with a bow. If harvesting an animal is your only concern, you must get this idea out of your head to be a truly sincere bowhunter.

☐ A person can be an excellent hunter with a firearm but this does not mean that he / she will be one with a bow and arrow. Attitudes must change as well as hunting methods and for the most part the gun hunting mentality must be removed. Learn as much as you can about the animal that you wish to harvest and the land that it inhabitats. Using this information to your advantage can indeed be successful.

☐ Much of the public does not understand game management. Bow hunting is a high recreation, low harvest yield sport and as such brings in much revenue to the province which in turn goes into wildlife rehabilitation projects and conservation efforts. We do not see anti-hunters and environmentalists putting in the money that hunters do to properly manage our game species. There are just too many bleeding hearts out there with the intent to save a species by fighting the hunting issue. The question that one must ask the animal rights activist is what makes them think that they have more knowledge about hunting and game management than the game wardens and biologists who are paid by the government They are trained to control our game species. If there is no control over the populations, the species would get diseases and/or starve to death because of high population numbers and low food supply. High population numbers would also cause an increase in predators which would cause insurmountable problems to the human population and put many people at risk. Contrary to what the activist thinks, it is better to be humanely taken with an arrow or a bullet than to starve to death or be eaten alive by predators.

☐ Look at all the predator species that are out there. The predators have eyes in their head that face forward. This is so that they can concentrate on their prey. The prey has eyes which are along the side of their head so that they can observe more in a larger field of vision. In this manner they are given extra vision to spot the predators. Now, look at a human being. Our eyes face the front like a predator. God meant for us to be a predator.

☐ Animal rights activists although they mean well, do not understand the role of the hunter. We as hunters should refrain from using terms like kill, wound, stick or maim. In order to give the bowhunter more respect and to show reverence for the animal, try using terms like: harvest, or take. That is in effect what we are doing.

☐ Another thing that the animal rights activists have a field day with is the term, "trophy hunting". This term implies that the animal is taken just for its head gear or skull size. This is wrong. Any animal taken with a bow and arrow is a trophy and the trophy is in the eyes of the beholder. Any animal harvested by bow or gun should be utilized to its fullest and it is up to you the hunter to determine which animal you wish to harvest. Try to stay away from the term "trophy hunting". It leaves a bad taste in everybody's mouth and does nothing but belittle the hunter.

From The Lord's Book

☐ From the moral aspect, all hunting including bowhunting is a necessary product of humanity. For those of you who are religious, You will note that there are many quotes within the bible where the good Lord has given mankind permission to hunt and eat meat. The animal rights activists disregard these quotes as they do not fall into what they perceive as being the right thing to do. As bowhunters we must realize that we are doing the right thing by hunting and that this activity falls into Gods grand scheme of things.

RELIGIOUS QUOTES THAT GIVE MAN PERMISSION TO HUNT

☐ Genesis 9, Verse 3: When God said unto Noah: "All moving things that liveth shall be meat to you. Even as the green herb, I have given you all things".

☐ Genesis 27, Verse 3: " Now, therefore take, I pray thee, thy weapons, thy quiver and thy bow and go into the field and **Take** some venison."

☐ Should man hunt? Genesis 27:3; 9:2; Leviticus 17:13 says yes.

☐ Is killing wrong? God gives us permission to harvest animals but not to take the life of a man. Genesis 9;3, 9;6

☐ Animals on the same level as man? NO They were not made in the likeness of God. Genesis 1:27; 9:6 Ecclesiastes 3:21

☐ In Genesis 9:2 It is said while speaking of animals :Into your hand they have been delivered.

☐ For those of you who have trouble convincing the gun hunter as to the effectiveness of the bow and arrow. Why not try this. Fill a five gallon plastic pail with sand and have your gun hunter friend fire a round into it with his firearm. The caliber will not make a difference. Even if he wants to go as high as a 375 H&H magnum. Then fire an arrow at the pail. He will probably be surprised to find out that the arrow will penetrate farther if not through the pail of sand. His bullet will hardly penetrate at all.

☐ Most of the time animals that were harvested by a bow and arrow are more tender eating then those harvested by a firearm. The reason is that because the firearm kills by shock and impact. When the animal is hit it tenses up causing Adrenalin to surge through its body. The heart stops and the blood remains in most of the meat. When a animal is harvested with a arrow the shock is not as severe and the heart continues to pumps the blood out of and into the cavity of the animal. When this happens the blood flows out of the veins in the meat which in turn is the same type of bleeding that is done in slaughter houses. The animals when bled out causes the meat to be more tender.

CHAPTER FOUR
Clothes For The Bowhunter

CLOTHES FOR THE BOWHUNTER

Without getting into some brand names in this chapter there are several things that we as bowhunters must think of when we are looking for hunting clothes. This chapter is printed for the benefit of those who are thinking of purchasing a new outfit or just replacing some of the older worn out clothes that you now have. In doing this we will start from the head and work down.

SPRING AND FALL

☐ Hat: My best recommendation is the roll up hat. This hat was used in the jungles of Vietnam and is suitable for the use of bowhunting for the following reasons.
The brim usually is about two or three inches which is enough to keep the sun out of your eyes and also is short enough that it does not interfere with your bowstring when you pull it back to release the arrow. This is a common problem when one wears a baseball type hat. This hat has a brim that goes entirely around the hat and in doing so allows the water to run down the hat and away from the back of the neck when it rains. Another benefit of the roll up hat is that you can cover your head over the hat with a mosquito head net. By doing this the brim of the hat keeps the net away from your head, neck and face. Once the net is tucked into the top of your camo suit the black flies etc. cannot get at you.

FACE CAMO: Painting yourself up with the camo paints I think is a messy business. Your best bet is to use a spanoflage face mask or one of the others on the market. These do a great job of hiding your face and are relatively cheap. They can usually be purchased at any sporting goods store that sells bowhunting equipment or army surplus supplies.

THINGS THAT GIVE YOU AWAY AS A HUNTER: SHINE, SHAPE, SIZE, SMELL, SILHOUETTE, SOUND AND MOVEMENT

☐ CAMOUFLAGE: When looking for camo clothing the following things should be kept in mind. The clothes should be quiet as you are hunting with a close quarters weapon and silence is important. A camouflage pattern should be picked that will best suit the majority of the terrain that you intend to hunt in. I have one suit which is patterned woodland camo for hunting in fir trees, one that is world war two pattern which is great for poplar trees and one white for snow and skyline pattern.

I would recommend full coveralls as there is a greater amount of warmth that can be achieved in these. There is less of a chance for insects and flies to enter the clothes and have you for dinner.

Look for a suit that has ample zippers so you can use them as vents to cool yourself down if needed.

Check the suit for breast pockets. If they have flaps on them they may get in the way of your bowstring upon release. Add a few Velcro strips on the cuffs and ankles as well as on the arms of your bow hand. This is to pick up any slack in the clothing and stop your bowstring from hitting it.

Look for a suit that is easy to wash and dry and does not soak up water like a sponge. If possible try to find a suit with a hood that has a drawstring. Some suits have extra patches on the elbows and knees and this makes it more rugged and hence last longer.

☐ HANDS: Wearing camo paint on your body is effective but very messy. Your hands should be covered as they move around a lot and you might as well wave a flag. The next best answer is gloves. There are two routes to go here. The thick glove which although hot is also the answer for flies or the spanoflage light gloves which keep your hands cool yet camouflages them adequately. Thinsulate has made a mitt style glove and the mitt section is easily removed from the fingers for shooting. The mitt section has a Velcro strip which fastens itself to the back of the hand and is extremely quiet.

SHARE YOUR HARVEST WITH THE LANDOWNER

☐ FOOTWEAR: Because the animals that we hunt have such excellent senses and smell being one of them, rubber boots should top the list. For some reason animals cannot smell rubber. In warm weather a simple pair of green hunting boots should do it and if it gets cooler then you should consider boots that have a felt liner in them and ones that are comfortable to walk in as well as give you lots of warmth while sitting in your treestand.

WINTER

☐ SWEATER: With the cold your clothes have to change. I prefer to wear a wool toque the color of the camo suit that I am wearing at the time of the hunt. For close up treestand or ground blind work I find that the balaclava is the answer. I particularly like the one that has the eye holes and mouth hole in them. In this way I am keeping warm and hiding my face. In the snow the white ones are preferred and in the cold weather with no snow the camo or green colored ones are best. the mouth hole allows you to breathe freely without getting the face wet from moisture from your breath.

TO SCENT PROOF YOUR HUNTING CLOTHES PUT THEM IN A SCENT FREE PLASTIC BAG WITH BAKING SODA.

☐ LOOK FOR QUIET INSULATED CAMO COVERALLS: Deep pockets allow you ample space to put hand warmers in and your hands as well. They should be roomy yet not bulky. Again watch out for breast pockets. As the sleeves on these suits can sometimes be bulky it is sometimes an idea to cut the toe out of a sock and pull it over your bow arm so that the bowstring will not hit it on your release. This is sort of a makeshift arm guard. Make sure that the suit has a hood with a drawstring as it can get pretty cold sitting in a tree in below zero weather. I would highly recommend that a bowhunter practice regularly with his equipment, dressed in these coveralls as it is a different type of shooting. Usually one has to pay big bucks for suits like this so try to find one that is reversible with two different colors of camo to it.

☐ MITTS OR GLOVES: Wool is still a good pick but Thinsulate is a good choice as well. Because you want to have finger access. Look for a mitt which has gloves in them with the fingers cut out. These gloves also have a mitt sock which flips over the fingers when you do not have to shoot and they keep your hands pretty warm until you flip the sock back up to shoot.

OBTAIN LANDOWNERS PERMISSION

☐ BOOTS: In the winter and cold it is best to get a water proof boot that has felts and several liners in them. When standing on a metal stand it is pretty easy for the cold to transfer from the metal to the boot. Further into this book in, "Gift Ideas for Bowhunters" I have more information which indicates the best winter boots that I have found to date.

When the weather is really cold a bowhunter has to be careful that he does not bury himself in heavy clothes.

A good pair of long underwear followed by pants, a T-shirt and sweater should be sufficient if you have a superior set of coveralls and good boots. Sometimes your rear end can get pretty cold sitting in the tree for long hours. If this is the case one could consider an insulated seat pad. If you do use one of these make sure that it is secured to the treestand seat so that it does not fall off when you stand up.

CHAPTER FIVE
Gifts For The Bowhunter

"The Jungle Cat"
A man out standing in his field
..96..

GIFTS FOR YOUR BOWHUNTER
TRIED & TRUE

Many hunters and their spouses have come to me wanting to know what kind of equipment etc. they should buy themselves and their loved ones for bowhunting. The requests were so many that I have decided to put some information in this book. This is so that they too can benefit from the years of hunting experience, trials and errors that I have gone through to pick up this information

It would seem that the main times I get these calls are before hunting season, someone's birthday and at Christmas. Here in Canada it is not always easy to get bowhunting and archery related equipment so where possible I will tell you what the equipment is and where to get it to the best of my knowledge.

The equipment that I am going to mention are items that I personally have tried and feel that I can easily endorse. I am confident that they are among some of the best available. Also in presenting these items I will give you a description of these items as well as some of the benefits that they have to offer.

For those of you who are bowhunters and want to give your spouse a hint about what you want for a present, why not let your mate read this section and tick off the items in the small squares to the right that you wish to obtain? ..97..

☐ **Treestand**: Even though I have the body of a Chip & Dale dancer it has been said that I am a little over weight. At 275 pounds and 6'1", I was looking for a treestand that would take my weight, would be easy to set up, comfortable, light weight and quiet.

I have tried just about every treestand available and the only one that I have found that fits all of these requirements was the *Screaming Eagle.*

The stand has a seat on it which is 25" high, enough that your legs are not bent at the knees at any major angle and it is very comfortable on the legs allowing you to sit comfortably for long periods of time. When you stand up, the padded seat is in such a position that it rises quietly with you by means of your leg pressure and it folds easily upwards alongside the tree trunk out of the way. When you want to sit down, the seat easily and quietly moves back down into its sitting position with little pressure from your butt on the seat.

The platform is large 24" x 25" wide although it is very lightweight. In its original advertising I saw this stand tied to a tree holding up a Volkswagon bug and another time it held up several elk at once. These animals and the Volkswagon bug were tied to the end of the stand and it took the weight with ease.

The stand is carried up the tree to the desired position and a rubber coated chain is used to wrap around the tree and is secured to the stand by a hook which holds the chain and stand in place. Although not necessary, I wrap the chain through the treestand again and around the tree and lock it in place through the chain loops as I feel more secure knowing that if someone finds it, stealing it would be more difficult.

This is a benefit that many stands do not have as they are tied to the tree by belts and ropes. This stand comes with a bow holder and a rubber dipped chain, options which I would strongly recommend that you purchase with your stand. The bow holder is a simple item which can be placed for left or right hand shooters. Your bow when placed in it, is in easy reach with little movement .

The stand weighs about 14 pounds. Unfortunately these stands are not sold in Canada yet, however, if you wish to purchase one you can contact;
Screaming Eagle 100 Greensburg Rd. New Kensington, P.A. U.S.A. 15068 1-412-339-2352, 1-800-458-2017 Cost U.S. Price $135.00

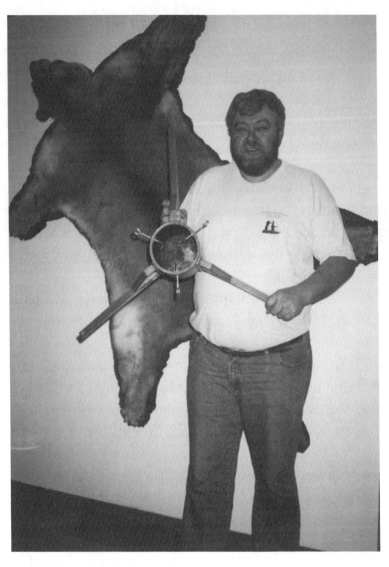

I asked for a Treestand one Christmas, this is what I got

..100..

☐ **Boots**: In the northern parts of Canada it can be cold enough to freeze the broadheads off of your arrows. I have hunted in Northern Quebec near Ungava Bay, In the tundra, swamp and freezing bog of Northern Ontario, The Yukon, Northern Saskatchewan, British Columbia and in the Territories. During these hunts I have spent many hours in a treestand as well as walking the turf. When it comes to getting cold feet the term, "Been there, done that"' applies to me.

One of the key difficulties that I have found when sitting on my stand is that my feet will eventually get cold while they are standing on the metal platform of the treestand. This is especially critical when hunting whitetails in the snow and while hunting trails and scrapes in the winter months.

Here in B.C., the seasons end around the 25 th of December in some places for deer and then cougar season goes well into January. When hunting in Northern Saskatchewan from a treestand you can really freeze your feet with the wind and chill factor going down to 50 to 70 below zero.

Kaufman has made a new boot which I have found more than adequate for this purpose. They even advertise this *Sorel* boot as a treestand boot. I have never seen that before so I know that they know what we as hunters are up against. Their *Glacier* boot comes in three colors that I am aware of, Black, Blue and Charcoal.

From the hunters stand point, in the treestand I would recommend the Charcoal ones as they tend to blend in with the color of the tree more. Blue is an easy color to pick out in the trees and black is noticeable but not as prevalent as blue. These boots have deep treads which lift your boot bottom off of the metal platform. They then have an insole pad which fits inside the bottom of the boot and then there is a sweat pad insole which fits on top of that. There is a felt liner which goes in and then there is another insole that fits inside of the felt liner. The outer boot has a canvas outer cover which is tied up and stops just below your knees. The top can also be tied off and this prevents snow from going in, melting and getting you wet. Let me tell you, these puppies are made for bowhunters who want to stay in their stands all day. You had better bring your pee jug with you because you will not want to leave your stand.

You only need one pair of socks when you wear these boots. I would however recommend that you pull all of the felts and insoles out at night when you go to bed so that they are nice, dry and comfortable in the morning.

I picked these boots up at *Marks Work Wear House* and they are available all over Canada. However, In the United States they can be purchased from *Cabelas.*

If you wish to get more information about them or want to order some you can contact Kaufman Footwear, P.O. Box 9005 Kitchener, Ontario, N2G4J8 1-(519)-576-1500 Cost in 1996 was about $119.00 Canadian

WHEN HUNTING CLOSE, CAMO PAYS OFF

☐ **Camouflage Suits:** As I mentioned earlier, bowhunting in Canada can get pretty cold. With this in mind I was looking for a good quality camo suit which offer colors for winter and fall hunting. I also wanted something which would be easy to put on and take off and at the same time not interfere with the motions of pulling back my bow. I wanted something that was extremely quiet, had a hood and something that was big enough to hold my perfect body when I was wearing long johns, pants, sweaters etc.

As I needed a big size I was also handicapped in that dept. as well. After trying many different styles of suit I came upon the *Skyline Camo Company*. The suit that I purchased from them was reversible, a combination snow camo (which they call *skyline*) and tree camo coveralls. I find that coveralls are best as there is no blast of cold air rushing up your back when you bend over or sit down. This suit is insulated as well as, if not better than one of our good quality Canadian snow suits. Believe it or not these suits come in sizes up to 5X large and extra tall.

This is something that you rarely see as most companies think that only midgets are bowhunters. They have a hood which is also reversible and buttons so it is easy to remove if you so desire. The suit has zippers which start at the bottom of each leg and go up quite high much like our northern ski doo suits. It also has vent type opening in the sides with which you can gain easy access to your pants pockets or just simply to help you cool down a bit. There is of course a zipper which runs down the front of the suit and all the zippers are two way ones which comes in handy for when mother nature calls upon you to do your thing. (Not near your treestand I hope)

I have had hundreds of deer and other species as well look up at me in my tree while wearing the *Skyline* snow winter camo. They didn't even make me out and some were right under the treestand. This suit is very warm and it brushes off the cold like butter on a hot hunting knife. There was one thing that concerned me when I purchased the suit and that was that it had a breast pocket. I feared that the bow string would hit it upon my release and I decided to cut the flap off if it interfered with the shooting, but after 10 years of use it has not happened yet. So far the pocket has been saved. I think that it is the positioning of the pocket which keeps it just out of the way.

Cost of this coverall runs from $139.00 to $151.00 U.S. The hood is an option

These suits can be purchased in the United States from: *Skyline Camouflage Inc*. 184 Ellicott Road, West Falls, New York U.S.A. 14170 Phone # 1-(716)-655-0230 or 1-800-997-7955. Fax # 1-(716)-655-3874

When I contacted *Skyline* and asked for permission to mention their name they offered a 10% U.S. discount to any person who makes a purchase over $100.00 U.S. from them and sends in the coupon at the rear of "The Bowhunter's Tip Book." (Pretty neat eh)

As a point of interest the camo pattern on the outside cover of this book is also one of *Skylines*.

"OH MY GOD, HE SHOT A DOE!"

Proof That Anything That You Take With Your Bow Is A Trophy

☐ **Face mask**: In cold weather hunting it is best to keep your face and head warm at all times. Your head acts like a chimney with the heat escaping your body when there is nothing on top of it. When you lose this heat you will start to get cold. When I go hunting in the cold and wear my skyline snow camo I like to wear a balaclava that is white as it blends in with the rest of the outfit. A balaclava can be purchased at any ski shop and a wool one is very comfortable and warm. To save yourself a few bucks you can try to get your wife to knit you one for a Christmas present. Cost in Canadian prices about $9.95

There is another product on the market which is extremely comfortable and easy to wear. The spanoflage head net has a solid cloth top which stops the heat from leaving your head area and thereby keeps the warmth in your body. The net clings close to your face and is made almost like a screen which in turn cuts down on the shiny areas of your face. One can see through the material however you can cut out eye and mouth holes to give you better vision. These items come in various colors and run at about $9.95 each. They can be picked up at most sporting goods stores in Canada and the U.S.

☐ **Flashlight**: Without a doubt the little **mini mag** flashlight is probably the favorite of most bowhunters. It's light weight and small six inch size makes it easy to carry in or out of your hunting area. The light has an indentation at the end of the handle into which you can thread a piece of cord to wrap around your wrist so that it is more difficult to lose. The mini-mag throws a bright beam of light out and easily shows you the way in or out of your treestand. When used in conjunction with reflective type thumb tacks to mark your way the mini-mag will show you what direction to take. The light weighs several ounces and takes two pen light batteries to operate. The batteries do not wear down fast either. Although not related to bowhunting, when I was on the Police Force I always carried a **mini mag** and I once had to use it in the cold for traffic control when my issued flashlight broke down. The driving public had no trouble seeing me or understanding my signals as I used the little light. The handle is knurled and this makes it easy to hold and will not slip when you are using it to clean your animal in the dark.

I do not know if this was the intended purpose but when I am in the cabin and the outhouse and there is no lantern available I unscrew the cap off of the bulb end of the flashlight and the light comes on and spreads itself out to light up the whole room. The small flashlight also has a spare bulb which comes with it when you purchase it.

The bulb is inside the back of the flashlight behind the batteries. Spare bulbs seem to be easy to obtain and there is no maintenance required on these units. There seems to be several different kinds of cases that they come in and all of them fit unto your belt. I have found that the best case to purchase is the one that has a Velcro flap which folds over the top of the light and secures it in place. I have lost several lights which have been put in a case with no flap on it and would not recommend buying that kind. These flashlights show others up and are available all over the United states and Canada in sporting goods stores and department stores everywhere.

Costs run from $16.95 to $19.95 Canadian in 1996.

☐ **Jack knife**: What I have always looked for in a knife is one that is compact, holds an edge and is easy to hold with a good grip. The knife must have a carrying case that is not bulky and light so that when wearing it you would not even realize that it is there. This I like, as it really bothers me when my knife with its case gets caught up in the camo coveralls that I am wearing.

My prayers to the perfect knife answering this description were answered when **Buck** came out with their **Buck Light knife.** The knife comes in a small, light but not bulky cloth case which fits close to your body yet offers you no feeling that it is there. The top of the case is closed with a Velcro seal. The overall length of the knife is seven

inches when opened and it sports a three inch blade which when sharpened can keep an edge up with the best of them. The buck light is only four inches in length when folded. This knife is excellent for all camping and hunting uses and has no problem holding its own when cutting open your animals body cavity or taking the hide off of your deer. The **Buck light** knife is found throughout Canada and the United States at any dealer that sells **Buck** knives. A person would have no problem finding an outlet which sells them.
Average cost in Canadian prices in 1996 $35.00

☐ **Arrows:** There are many types of arrows available with the types being aluminum, fiberglass, carbons and wood. My preference is wood shafts as I like to make my own arrows from scratch. These arrows are extremely tough and contrary to popular belief they fire extremely well out of compound bows. They are much cheaper to make and shoot. The spines are the same for a compound as they are for recurves and longbows. One can buy the arrows already made from some of your local arrow makers at a reasonable price. Many people including myself will buy arrow shafts in groups of 100's at a cheaper rate. You then only need to purchase feathers, nocks, stain, paint and glue and you can make your own up for half the price. I have hunted with a bow for over twenty years and went through all the makes of arrows.

To this day wood is still my preference. Wood shafts can be obtained from: Wolverine Manufacturing P.O. Box #333 Vanderhoof, British Columbia V0J3A0 1-(250)-567-4651 Cost for 100 shafts is $65.00 Canadian in 1996.

☐ **Broadhead sharpener**: I have been through it all, cut fingers, cursing files, replaceable blades, leather straps and ceramic sharpeners. Finally I came across the answer for sharp broadheads. The **Mastercraft "Wet Sharpener"**. This is a light motor driven sharpener which has a 170 RPM. The grinding wheel on it is perfect for sharpening your broadheads and your hunting knives. I would recommend this sharpener for fixed heads only and not replaceable blades. These you have to buy. When sharpening the heads I also put an edge on the back blades and this job is handled with no problem by the wet stone. You have to add a small cup of water to the stone as you run it and you have easy access to all the angles that you need to sharpen your arrow heads. This unit plugs into a regular household socket and has a two way switch which allows you to run your wet stone forwards or reverse. To date this is the best answer to my prayers for both razor sharp broadheads and knives.

KEEP YOUR KNIVES AND BROADHEADS SHARP
Mastercraft tools are sold in Canada and in the United

States and I purchased mine from Canadian Tire. The regular price in 1996 was $60.00 Canadian, however, for two years in a row now at Christmas time they have been on sale for $39.95 Canadian.

☐ **Broadheads:** I am a firm believer that fixed broadheads are the best, toughest and most economical broadheads on the market. Even though you have to sharpen them you Can use the heads over and over again. My favorite choice is the *Magnus II* broadhead. This head has two blades which has a one and one quarter inch cutting diameter. I personally like to sharpen the back blades on them giving me the ultimate cutting edge possible. They are a fixed head and the *Magnus II* weighs 125 grains.

Let me tell you how tough they are. I have harvested a whitetail, mule deer and a moose all with the same head. I resharpened it each time although after each deer harvested I didn't have to. The moose was shot at 15 yards and the arrow was a pass through and I lost it. I am sure that I could have used the same head again had I found it.

In December 1994 I shot at and missed a deer and I found the arrow in November of 1996. The head which I had lightly coated with Vaseline was not rusted and was still

as sharp as the day I fired it. This head spent two full winters and three summers stuck in the wet ground. The broadheads come in packs of six.
They are made and can be ordered from: **Magnus Archery** Company P.O. Box 1877, Great Bend, KS. U.S.A. 67530 1-(316)-793-9222
In Canada you can order them from:
Golden Arrow Archery P.O. Box 1652, Regina, Saskatchewan F4P3C4 1-(306)-757-1221

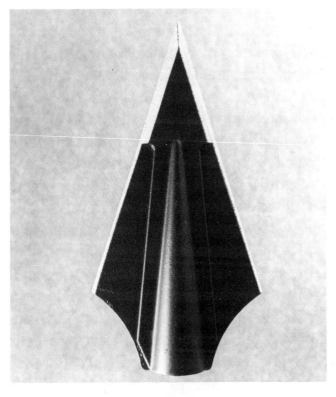

Scents: There are several makes of scents on the market today and they fall into several different categories. Those being: sex, food, cover scent or masking scent and attractants. It is extremely important to remember that certain scents must be used at certain times of the year and under certain conditions. It would not be smart to use a sex scent for whitetails during a time of year that they have no sexual interest. In the case of scents. I have tried most of them and to this date the most effective sex scent that I have found during the start to the end of the rut period are the *James Valley Scents.*

These scent gels are extremely efficient when hunting scrapes and I highly recommend them. What makes *James Valley Scents* so unique is that there is only a certain amount made and then that is it for the year. They also have available to the hunter an informative pamphlet which tells you what to look for, where to place it and how to apply it. The scent gel comes in a 1 ounce small glass bottle and they suggest that you keep the scent in a cool place when not in use. I have personally shot two bucks off of the same scrape using this scent gel in the pre rut. The scent is available at most sporting goods stores and many times you must ask them to order it in for you. In Canada I have paid $12.95 for it and when I find some I pick it up right away. This scent is made and sold in the U.S. by : *James Valley Scents* HCR 1, Box 47 Mellette, South Dakota U.S.A. 57461

Deer Grunt Tube: Grunt tubes are an excellent tool when used at the proper time. To use a grunt tube in early September is not feasible or effective.

It is best during the to use it pre rut, rut and post rut period. For those of you who doubt its use, I had shot a whitetail doe and left her on the trail where she fell because I had another whitetail tag left. A small herd of five deer came along the trail and stopped at the dead deer. I had accidentally coughed in my treestand and the five deer slowly turned around and retraced their footsteps. I quietly blew on the grunt tube and all five deer turned around and walked past the expired doe and came right under my treestand.

This was in the post rut period and the sound imitates the sound of a buck deer.

These grunt tubes can be purchased at any sporting goods store and they all seem to be effective.

A grunt tube can be purchased for anywhere from $5.00 to $12.00 Canadian

Another item is a book called *Deer Talk.* This book is very informative and clearly explains the what to do's and the how to's of deer calling. The book can be ordered from E.L.K. Inc. P.O. Box 85 Gardiner, MT 59030 1-800-272-4355 and sells for $12.95 U.S. for paperback

☐ **Compact Saw:** These make great little gifts. When looking for them, try to find one that has two blades on it. One side of the blade is used for a meat saw with which you can cut meat and bone with and the blade on the other side is a wood cutting saw. This is used to clear branches from trees to make your treestand sit better and also to clear shooting trails. These saws are light and compact and can easily be strapped to your belt or placed in a fanny pack. These saws came under many names some of them being *Knapp saws, Pac saw*s and *Wyoming saws.* They can be purchased at any sporting goods store and usually run between $20.00 to $30.00 Canadian.

☐ **Bows**: As far as I am concerned bow preference is up to the individual.
I do not believe that it would be in your best interest to go out and buy a bow for someone else as a present. There are too many things that you must know about the individual in order to purchase a weapon that is suitable for them. How a bow feels, draw length, poundage that

the shooter can handle and personal preference of weapon should all be handled by the shooter themselves.

I would suggest that if this is what you want to purchase as a present for your hunter, buy them a gift certificate and let them get it themselves. Be careful when buying anything that you do not get caught up in the "load the bow up with gadgets syndrome" This is a common mistake and the hunter can actually be turned off by all the adjustments and complexities of our modern bows.

One should always remember that the more you load up on your bow the more it weighs and the more that can go wrong. Good bows can run from $200.00 to $2000.00 and most expensive does not mean best.

The Bowhunters Tip Book
and
Skyline Camouflage Inc.

*Are proud to offer you a discount for
purchasing this book*

For Mail Order Only

*Here's an unbelievable offer from Skyline Camouflage
designers of Apparition ™ -
Canada's hottest camo pattern!
With any purchase of over $100.00 U.S.
you will get a 10% U.S. discount.
Simply by sending this page to Skyline Camouflage*

If you require our free catalogue please let us know.

**SKYLINE CAMOUFLAGE INC.
184 Ellicott Road. West Falls, NY
U.S.A. 14170
1 - (716) - 665 - 0230
1 - (800) - 997 - 7955
Fax: 1-(716)-655-3874**

OH NO, NOT ANOTHER DOE!

IS THERE NO END?

The Bowhunters Tip Book
and
Screaming Eagle Inc.
proudly offer you this great savings.

Attention Hunters

To order a **Screaming Eagle Treestand** and receive a **10% U.S. discount** off of a brand new **Screaming Eagle Treestand.**
Simply cut out this page and send it in with your order to:

Screaming Eagle
100 Greensburg Rd.
New Kensington, PA.
U.S.A. 15068
1-(412)-339-2352

To order a catalogue containing the **Screaming Eagle** treestand and the many other bowhunting accessories, Simply give them a call or write and they will gladly assist you.

Bowhunters serving Bowhunters
..123..

If you wish to obtain additional copies of *The Bowhunters Tip Book*, *The Hunters Tip Book or The Inept Bowhunter*.

Please fill out the form below and sent it in with $12.95 Canadian or $9.95 U.S. per book. Add $1.75 for one book and $2.75 for two or more books for shipping and handling to.

B.S. Publications
P.O. Box 2053
Kelowna, British Columbia
V1X4K5

Name: ....

Address: ....

City/Town: ....

Province/State: .... Postal/Zip Code: ....

Please check off: *The Bowhunter's Tip Book* ( )
    The Hunter's Tip Book ( ) *The Inept Bowhunter* ( )

Certified Cheque or Money Order please
U.S. Orders must be in U.S. Funds.

The Inept Bowhunter is a book which is put together from a combination of short stories that have occurred to Bob Marchand as a bowhunter while attempting to harvest game animals. This humorous yet practical book puts out the stories the way it was seen through the eyes of this bowhunter. In several areas of the book there are some How To's which could be of use to persons who wish to pick up extra hints in pursuit of game.

The photos throughout this book are both comical and serious. This is a must read for anyone with a sense of humor and a yearn to learn.